SCHIRMER'S LIBRARY
OF MUSICAL CLASSICS

Vol. 2097

T0071658

JACQUES-FÉRÉOL MAZAS

Twelve Little Duets, Op. 38
For Two Violins
Books 1 and 2

Edited and Fingered by Henry Schradieck

ISBN 978-1-4584-2108-1

G. SCHIRMER, Inc.

DISTRIBUTED BY

HAL•LEONARD®
CORPORATION
7777 W. BLUEMOUND RD. P.O. BOX 13819 MILWAUKEE, WI 53213

www.schirmer.com
www.halleonard.com

CONTENTS

Twelve Little Duets
Op. 38, Book 1

Jacques-Féréol Mazas
(1782–1849)

VIOLIN 1

VIOLIN 1

VIOLIN 1

VIOLIN 1

VIOLIN 1

RONDO
Allegretto

VIOLIN 1

VIOLIN 1

VIOLIN 1

RONDO
Allegretto

VIOLIN 1

VIOLIN 1

VIOLIN 1

VIOLIN 1

VIOLIN 1

SCHIRMER'S LIBRARY
OF MUSICAL CLASSICS

Vol. 2097

JACQUES-FÉRÉOL MAZAS

Twelve Little Duets, Op. 38
For Two Violins
Books 1 and 2

Edited and Fingered by Henry Schradieck

ISBN 978-1-4584-2108-1

G. SCHIRMER, Inc.

DISTRIBUTED BY

HAL•LEONARD®
CORPORATION
7777 W. BLUEMOUND RD. P.O. BOX 13819 MILWAUKEE, WI 53213

www.schirmer.com
www.halleonard.com

CONTENTS

VIOLIN 2

Twelve Little Duets
Op. 38, Book 1

Jacques-Féréol Mazas
(1782–1849)

VIOLIN 2

VIOLIN 2

VIOLIN 2

RONDO
Allegretto

VIOLIN 2

VIOLIN 2

RONDO
Allegretto

VIOLIN 2

VIOLIN 2

VIOLIN 2

VIOLIN 2

Allegro moderato

5.

VIOLIN 2

VIOLIN 2

VIOLIN 2

VIOLIN 2

Twelve Little Duets
Op. 38, Book 2

Jacques-Féréol Mazas
(1782–1849)

VIOLIN 2

VIOLIN 2

VIOLIN 2

9. Allegro

ROMANCE
Andante

DANSE NÈGRE
Allegretto

A

VIOLIN 2

VIOLIN 2

PASTORALE
Andante

VIOLIN 2

RONDO
Allegretto

Allegro maestoso

12.

VIOLIN 2

VIOLIN 2

VIOLIN 2

TRIO

D.C. al ⊕ senza repetizione, e poi la Coda

CODA

VIOLIN 1

Twelve Little Duets
Op. 38, Book 2

Jacques-Féréol Mazas
(1782–1849)

VIOLIN 1

VIOLIN 1

VIOLIN 1

ROMANCE
Andante

DANSE NÈGRE
Allegretto

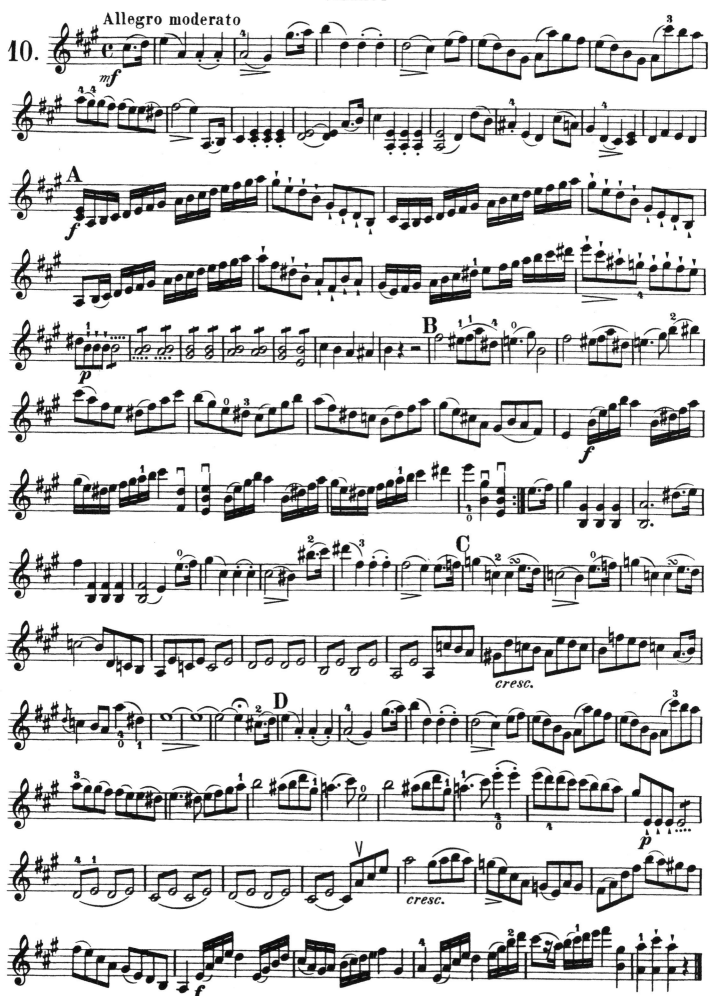

VIOLIN 1

VIOLIN 1

VIOLIN 1

RONDO
Allegretto

Allegro maestoso

12.

VIOLIN 1

VIOLIN 1

VIOLIN 1

TRIO

dol.

D.C. al ⊕ senza repetizione e poi la Coda

CODA